The Truth About
GOD'S RAINBOW

by Lisa Soland

The Truth About God's Rainbow
by Lisa Soland

Text copyright © 2020 Lisa Soland

CAUTION: All rights reserved. No part of this publication may be reproduced, stored in a retrieval system, or transmitted in any form or by any means electronic, mechanical, photocopy, recording, or other, except for brief quotations in written reviews, without the prior written permission of the publisher.

THE HOLY BIBLE, NEW INTERNATIONAL VERSION®, NIV® Copyright © 1973, 1978, 1984, 2011 by Biblica, Inc.™ Used by permission. All rights reserved worldwide.

Published in 2020 (softcover) and 2021 (hardcover) by:
Climbing Angel Publishing
PO Box 32381, Knoxville, Tennessee 37930
www.ClimbingAngel.com

First Edition of Hardcover, September 2021
Printed in the United States of America
Cover and Interior design by Climbing Angel Publishing
Cover print 7-themes.com

ISBN: 978-1-956218-14-5

This book is dedicated to my

beautiful sister, Linda.

The Truth About
GOD'S RAINBOW

A long time ago,
God went out looking for a person
who keeps their promises.

"Creation of the Sun, Moon, and Plants," by Fresco Cappella Sistina, 1511

He looked high.
And He looked low.

"Creation of Adam," by Michelangelo, 1508

But out of all the people living on the earth at that time,

God found only **one person** who fit that description.

His name was Noah.

And because Noah was a person who *kept his promises,*

God asked him to do something very difficult.

God asked Noah to build

a very, very, very,

VERY

large boat.

It wasn't easy to build a boat with that many **VERYS**

but Noah didn't care.

"Noah building the Ark,"
by Franzosischer Meister, 1675

He knew it was important

or God wouldn't
have asked him
to do it.

So, **to please God**

Noah did exactly what his heavenly Father asked and *built the boat.*

Pleasing God was enough of a reason for Noah to go ahead and do such a thing.

And to do **this** thing, it took Noah and his family 120 years.

120 YEARS to build God's boat!

Have you ever done anything for God that took that long?

Me neither.

"Illustration from the Nuremberg Chronicle," by Michael Wolgemut, Wilhelm Pleydenwurff, 1493

People would stop by and make fun of Noah but he was *patient and loving*, despite their grouchy moods.

Noah told them the truth. God was about to flood the earth and they needed to take a good look at all their wrong doings and tell God sorry, **AND REALLY MEAN IT.**

Because God knows when we ***really*** mean something or when we're just pretending.

Two of every kind of **bird**, **animal**, and **creeping** thing of the ground came to **Noah** so he could help keep them alive, which was also part of **God's plan.**

And when the boat was finished, **Noah** carefully led them all on board.

"Noah's Ark," by Edward Hicks, 1846

Then,

Noah asked his family,
very nicely,
to get on.

And they did. Thank God.

After over 120 years of preaching to all those people who heard Noah plainly speak the truth of what was about to happen, about how God loved them and didn't want them to perish, only eight people got on the boat.

Eight. That's all.

And when everyone and everything who *wanted* to be on the boat was on the boat,

God closed the door
and the rain began.

"The Entry of the Animals into Noah's Ark," by Jacopo Bassano, 1570

The fountains of the deep cracked open.

And if that wasn't enough,
    God tore open the ceiling of the great firmament
        and water gushed in from above.

You see, it had never rained on the earth before.
    This was the very first time
        and when God does a thing,
            he does it with excellence.

It rained hard for **40 days and 40 nights**.

It rained so hard that the water
piled up all around them
and turned into a flood that
covered the entire earth.

It was the **greatest flood** of all time.

And every living thing
that **was not** on that boat…

…*drowned.*

"The Great Flood," Bonaventura Peeters, 1st half of the 17th Century

Then, when the time was right,
God told the water to dry up and it did.

And everyone on that boat was very happy…

…because after spending **375** days and **375** nights on that boat, that boat didn't seem so very  after all…

…and they wanted OFF.

NOW.

"Noah's Ark on the Mount Ararat," by Simon de Myle, 1570

Noah was *in charge* so he was the happiest of all.

He was so happy that he built an altar to God and worshipped Him for
getting them off that boat.

(Being *in charge* is not easy.
That's why God has us pray for our leaders.)

"Noah and His Ark," by Charles Willson Peale, 1819

God promised Noah and his family

that he would **never** flood the entire world again.

Then God gave them a present
to remind them of that promise.

God gave them the **rainbow**, which He made.

"Noah Gives Thanks for Deliverance," by Domenico Morelli, 1901

But God didn't give the rainbow **only** to them
a long time ago.

He gave the rainbow to **you** and **me** too,
for today.

In fact, sometimes He gives it to us **twice**.

"Meteorology: a double rainbow," Colored lithograph by R.H. Digeon, 1868

So, when we see **a rainbow**

we think of **God**

and remember *His promise to us.*

Photo by Cheryl Empey

A smart **scientist**,
wearing a white lab coat,
might say that rainbows appear
when the sun is shining through
drops of water that fall from the sky.

Those drops of water

bend the light,

and then reflect it

back to your eye.

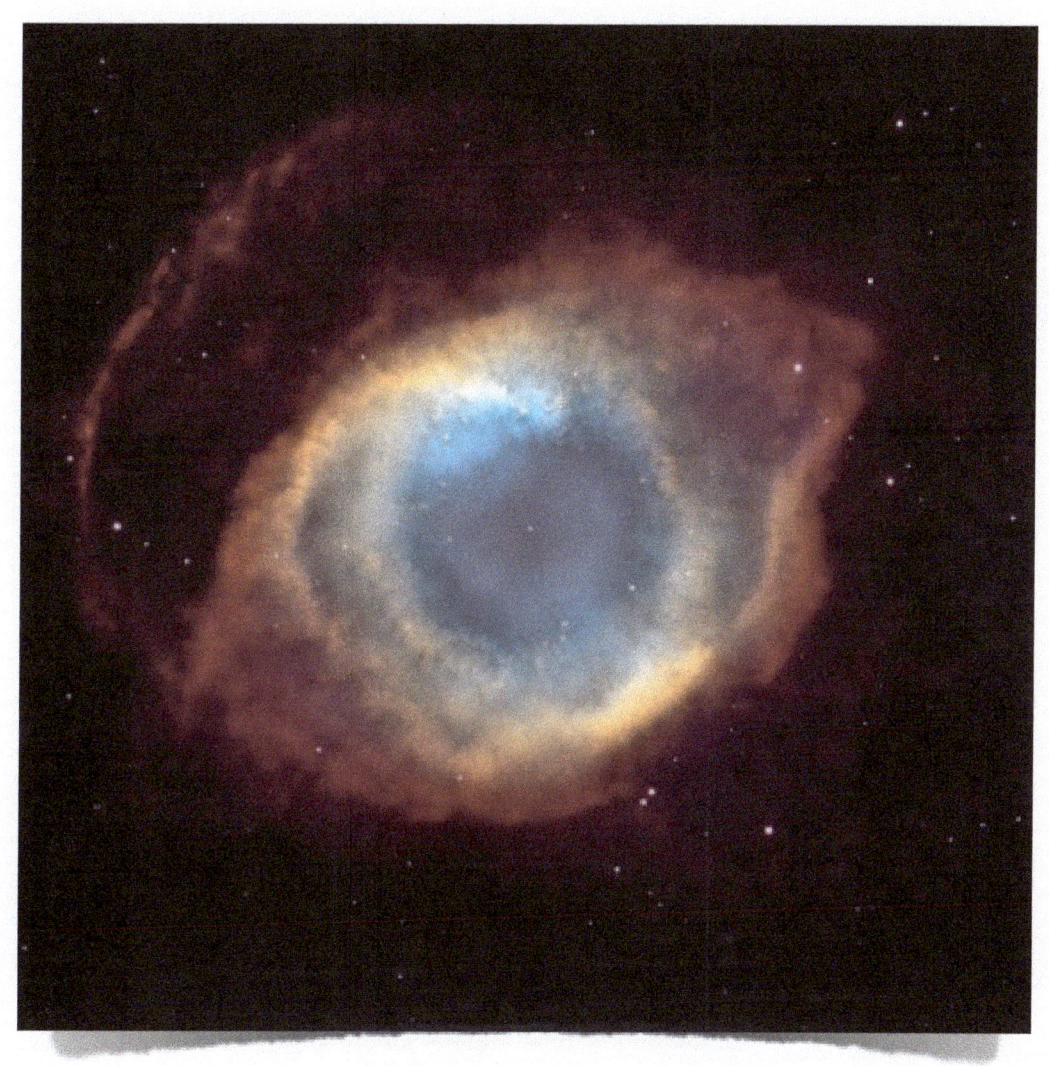

The **colors** show up differently
because each color is a different length,
due to the shape of a drop of rain,
which is a circle.

We only see the rainbow as *half of a circle*
because the horizon cuts off the other half.

"Rainbow in Devon, England," photo by Anna Langova

But as children of God
we **also** know that our Creator
makes **every part** of that rainbow.

God makes the rain
and the shape of a water droplet.

He made the sun,
He made your eye,
and He made **YOU!**

*(He even made that scientist
in the white lab coat.)*

In 1959, a *dashing* army captain by the name of **Ilhan Durupinar** found Noah's Ark in his country of **Turkey**.

It was up on a **very tall mountain**.

Scientists believe the large boat had been buried beneath a ton of hardened mud for a very long time.

And in 1948,
heavy rains and three earthquakes
shook the ground
and cracked open that ol' mud,
and Noah's Ark **suddenly reappeared**.

The boat had been there,
under the ground, for so very long
that the wood had turned to stone.
It petrified.

God kept that boat around for a reason,
maybe as another reminder
that **when God keeps a promise
He doesn't mess around**.

But we also have the beautiful rainbow.

And the rainbow appears from time to time
as a **reminder from God**
that no matter what happens
in this crazy, mixed up world,

God always keeps His promises.

And…

…He always keeps his promises because He loves us,
very, very, very, very, very, very, VERY much!

And that's a lot of **VERYS.**

"Whenever the rainbow appears in the clouds,
I will see it and remember

the everlasting covenant between God

and all living creatures

of every kind on the earth."

(Genesis 9:16)

The **very** end.

ABOUT CLIMBING ANGEL PUBLISHING

Climbing Angel Publishing exists for the purpose of sharing stories of hope and encouragement, aiding in the gathering together of community, and supporting the process of betterment. The following books are available at ClimbingAngel.com and major bookstores.

ADULT BOOKS: (Romans 8:28-30)

In His Image, Sam Polson (English, Romanian, & Mandarin)
By Faith, Sam Polson (English & Romanian)
My Birthday Gift to Jesus, Lisa Soland
Without Ceasing, Dr. Dennis Davidson
SonLight: Daily Light from the Pages of God's Word, Sam Polson
Corona Victus: Conquering the Virus of Fear, Sam Polson
Art Bushing: His Diary, Letters, & Photographs of WWII, Art Bushing
Art & Dotty: His Diary, Their Letters & Photographs of WWII, Art Bushing
Trimisul, Stan Johnson (Romanian)
Life Changing Prayer, Sam Polson

CHILDREN'S BOOKS: (Philippians 4:8)

The Christmas Tree Angel, Lisa Soland
The Unmade Moose, Lisa Soland
Thump, Lisa Soland
Somebunny To Love, Lisa Soland (English & Mandarin)
The Truth about God's Rainbow, Lisa Soland
God's Promises, Lisa Soland
The Boy & The Bagel Necklace, Lisa Soland
God's Hands and Feet, Lisa Soland
I Like To Be Quiet, Joni Caldwell
Wheels Off!, Karlie Saumier
Ella's Trip of a Lifetime, Melanie Ewbank
Because You Are Mine, Gayle Childress Greene
Jeremy Plays the Blues, Amy Oden Simpson
Bad Hair Day, Jasmyne Simpkins
I Like To Read, Joni Caldwell
Trunks Up!, Karlie Saumier
Ruby and the Treasure Within, Tonya Celeste Hobbs

www.ingramcontent.com/pod-product-compliance
Lightning Source LLC
Chambersburg PA
CBHW041229240426
43673CB00010B/286